DOGS

Amanda O'Neill

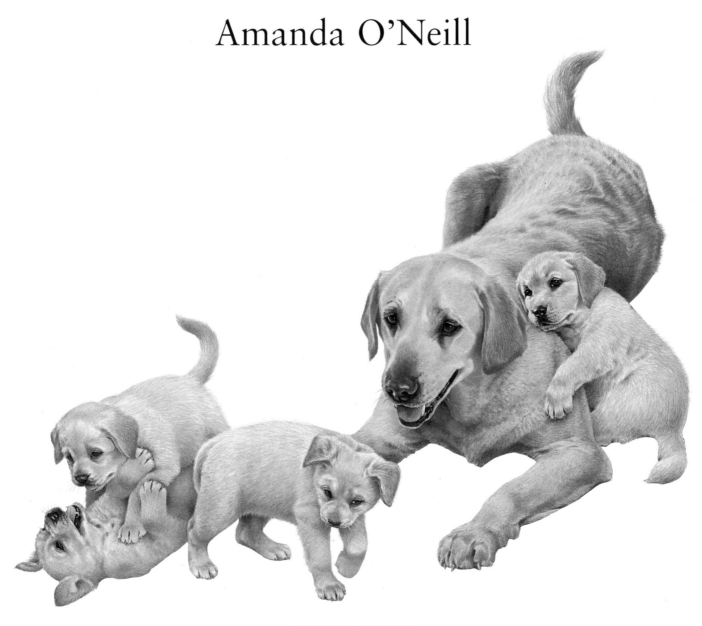

KING*f*ISHER

. NEW YORK

KINGFISHER
Larousse Kingfisher Chambers Inc.
95 Madison Avenue
New York, New York 10016

First published in hardcover in 1999
First published in paperback in 2001
10 9 8 7 6 5 4 3 (HC)
10 9 8 7 6 5 4 3 2 1 (PB)

1TR/1SCB/1100/GCUP/UNV/128CHST

LIBRARY OF CONGRESS CATALOGING-IN-PUBLICATION DATA
O'Neill, Amanda.
    Dogs / Amanda O'Neill.—1st ed.
        p. cm.
    Includes index.
    Summary: Introduces the physical characteristics and evolution of
dogs and describes different kinds of dogs and how to care for a dog
as a pet.
    1. Dogs—Juvenile literature. [1. Dogs.]   I. Title.
SF426.5.056   1999
636.7—dc21   98-39794   CIP   AC

ISBN 0-7534-5175-1 (HC)

ISBN 0-7534-5383-5 (PB)

Series editor: Sarah Allen
U.S. editor: Peggy Porter Tierney
Design: Ben White Associates
Art editor: Ch'en Ling
Picture manager: Jane Lambert
Picture researcher: Veneta Bullen
Cover illustration: David O'Connor, Chris Forsey
Cover design: Malcolm Parchment

Printed in Hong-Kong/China

CONTENTS

THE DOG FAMILY

Dogs vary in size, shape, and appearance more than any other animal species. For example, all cats, from a Siamese to a tiger, share a family resemblance. But dog breeds vary so much that it is hard to believe that a Mastiff and a Chihuahua belong to the same species.

▼ It's hard to choose between giants such as the Irish Wolfhound (1) and the Great Dane (2), or miniatures such as the Chihuahua (3) and the Dachshund (4), or between the shaggy Old English Sheepdog (5) and the naked Mexican Hairless (6). All of these dogs can be the best of companions, but it is important to choose a breed that will suit your own lifestyle.

For centuries, humans have taken advantage of the dog's adaptable design to develop different types of dogs for different jobs, such as hunting, guarding, or herding. Today, there are dogs with stumpy legs or stiltlike legs, heavy coats or none at all, long noses or flat faces, upright ears or floppy ears. But whatever its type, the dog has a long ancestry as "man's best friend."

▶ A Yorkshire Terrier only comes up to the ankles of a Mastiff, which may be more than one hundred times its size.

▶ Officially, the Chihuahua is the smallest breed, but a few Yorkies are smaller than any Chihuahua. Indeed, the record holder, which lived in the 1940s, was no bigger than a pack of cards.

Miacis

Cynodictus

The first dogs

Dogs' ancestry, like cats, bears, and other modern carnivores, can be traced back some 60 million years to a small, weasel-like beast called *Miacis*. The dog family began about 20 million years later with *Miacis*'s descendant, mongoose-like *Cynodictus*, to be followed by the first dog-like animal, *Hesperocyon*, or "Dawn Dog."

Hesperocyon ("Dawn Dog")

Bug hunter
In the tropical jungle of what is now North America, *Hesperocyon* hunted insects and small mammals on the forest floor. Short-legged and long-toed, it was still more mongoose than dog.

Canine cousins
Dog relatives, such as the jackal-like Dhole and badger-like Raccoon Dog, belong to separate branches of the family from true dogs and wolves.

Dhole

Raccoon Dog

PALEOCENE PERIOD
(65 to 55 million years ago)

EOCENE PERIOD
(55 to 38 million years ago)

OLIGOCENE PERIOD
(38 to 25 million years ago)

Bone crushers

Hyena Dogs, such as *Osteoborus*, were bear-like with bone-crushing teeth. They died out eight million years ago.

Dead ends

Many early members of the canine family, such as the Hyena Dogs, formed evolutionary dead-ends, leaving no descendants.

Osteoborus

Dogs' earliest ancestors were not very dog-like. Scurrying around forest floors or even climbing trees, they had yet to develop the speed to run down prey or the pack-hunting habits of modern dogs. But between seven and five million years ago, the Dawn Dog's descendants evolved into true dogs. Other branches of the family split off to develop into cousins of the modern dog and wolf—including the fox, the Raccoon Dog, and the Dhole.

Dire Wolf

Prairie runners

The way opened up for the evolution of true dogs when the spread of open grassland created a space for large, swift, grazing animals. To hunt such prey, early dogs began to develop the speed and pack-hunting techniques typical of modern dogs. The mighty Dire Wolf, now extinct, and our modern Gray Wolf both evolved about a million years ago.

Red Fox

Gray Wolf

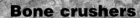

MIOCENE PERIOD
(25 to 5 million years ago)

PLEISTOCENE PERIOD
(2 million to 10 thousand years ago)

HOLOCENE PERIOD
(recent)

Wild dogs today

 Our domestic dog is just one member of a large, widespread family that also includes wild dogs, wolves, jackals, and foxes. The wolf, once found throughout most of Europe and North America, remains among the best-known members of the dog family, but today its range is greatly reduced.

► Wolves are family animals, sharing care of cubs and hunting together. Their social nature means that their descendant the dog is well adapted to accept a family role among humans.

Areas where the wolf is found

▲ The wolf used to roam much of the northern part of the world. But destruction of the wolf and its habitat by people means it is now restricted to the wilderness areas of North America and Asia, some forests of central and eastern Europe, and a few hilly areas of countries near the Mediterranean and in the Middle East.

Furry snowsuit
The Arctic Fox is well adapted to life in the frozen North. Its dense coat covers even the soles of its feet—vital protection in its harsh world of ice and snow.

Canine omnivore
Rudyard Kipling called the Golden Jackal, "the belly that runs on four feet," and, indeed, it eats absolutely anything, from bugs to fruit and vegetables.

Long legs
Nicknamed "the fox on stilts," the Maned Wolf is neither fox nor wolf. This South American canine hunts only small prey, from rodents to slugs and snails.

Winter sleeper
The Raccoon Dog is the only member of the dog family to hibernate in the winter. A native of the Far East, it has been introduced by humans into Eastern Europe.

The dog family can adapt to life almost anywhere, from the Arctic wastes to scorching deserts. Some members, such as the African Hunting Dog, are big, powerful hunters of large prey, while others, such as the Bat-eared Fox, are small insect eaters. Between them, the 32 wild species have settled every continent except Antarctica (though Australia's only wild dog, the Dingo, was actually introduced there centuries ago by primitive peoples). Today, hunting and, above all, habitat destruction have placed many of the world's wild dogs in danger of extinction.

Living with man
Many of the smaller wild dogs have learned that there are good pickings to be found where humans live. The Red Fox is common in many towns and even makes its home in the heart of some large cities. Parks and yards provide safe den sites, while fox restaurants abound in the form of garbage dumps, compost heaps, trash cans, and bird feeders.

▲ ▶ In ancient times, as now, dogs were children's playmates and guardians. Settlements were vulnerable to attack by animals and human raiders, so fierce dogs were valued for defense.

The dog's sense of family attached it strongly to its owners, as an ever-present companion, not just as a hanger-on. Dogs were also useful garbage disposals!

It did not take early man long to realize that the dog's hunting skills could be put to good use. Just as a wolf pack hunts cooperatively together, man and dog worked as a team to catch dinner.

From wolf to pet

The dog is not just man's best friend—it's probably our *oldest* friend! Archaeological evidence suggests that the dog was the first animal to be domesticated. Some of the oldest known remains date back to 10,000 B.C., but recent studies suggest that pet dogs may have been around even longer than that. Many dogs' ancestry can be traced back to wolves who lived 100,000 years ago, so some scientists regards that as the time when wolves must have begun to join human communities and grow more tame. Perhaps wolves were tamed by early man once the wolves had settled within foraging distance of village dumps. Over the years, the descendants of these tame wolves became something different. The key change was one of character rather than looks: the dog is essentially a wolf that never grows up, but remains dependent on its human family. A secondary change was the wide range of shapes and sizes that later developed. Breeds, such as the Greyhound and Mastiff, evolved at least 4,000 years ago. Today, wolves are rare—while dogs have become a success story.

▲ Hunters of the Zande tribe of central Africa train their Basenji dogs to drive game through the bush toward their nets. Because Basenjis don't bark, bells are put around their necks so their owners can hear where they are. This method of hunting is thousands of years old, as is the Basenji breed. Ancient Egyptian art from 2300 B.C. shows prick-eared, curly-tailed dogs, remarkably like the breed we know today.

▲ Australia's well-known "wild dog," the dingo, is actually a descendant of dogs introduced to the continent by humans, perhaps 4,000 years ago. In this Aborigine rock painting, the dingo is portrayed as one of the Aborigines' revered ancestors, accompanying the ancestor spirits of the human race.

Song dog

In the more remote parts of the world, native peoples still keep dogs of very ancient types. The American Indian Dog (nicknamed the "Song Dog" for its high voice) is a handsome example that closely resembles its wild cousin the coyote. Now rare, it was once kept widely by Native Americans from Canada to Mexico.

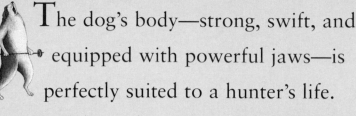

BODY TALK

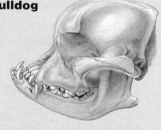
The dog's body—strong, swift, and equipped with powerful jaws—is perfectly suited to a hunter's life. Although domestic breeds have developed almost every variation of shape and size imaginable, the basic model is still recognizable underneath.

Pug

Bulldog

Mastiff

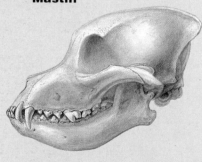

On your mark!

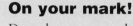
Dogs love to run, but compared with many other running animals, they are not among the fastest. The typical dog is built for staying power rather than high speed. A steady, energy-saving trot will carry it for many

Problems ahead

The head shapes of some modern breeds are not always very practical. Shortened skulls, such as the Pug's and Bulldog's, mean misplaced teeth and breathing problems. Compare them with the Mastiff's skull, which is closer to the wolf's long, strong head.

The short legs, flat nose, or barrel chest of many specially bred dogs mean they are not as well equipped to survive in the wild as their ancestor, the wolf. Bulldogs, for example, often suffer from a range of health problems.

Legging it

Dogs' legs are designed for long-distance running. The bones are usually long, although some specially bred dogs, such as Dachshunds, have been selected for their very short legs.

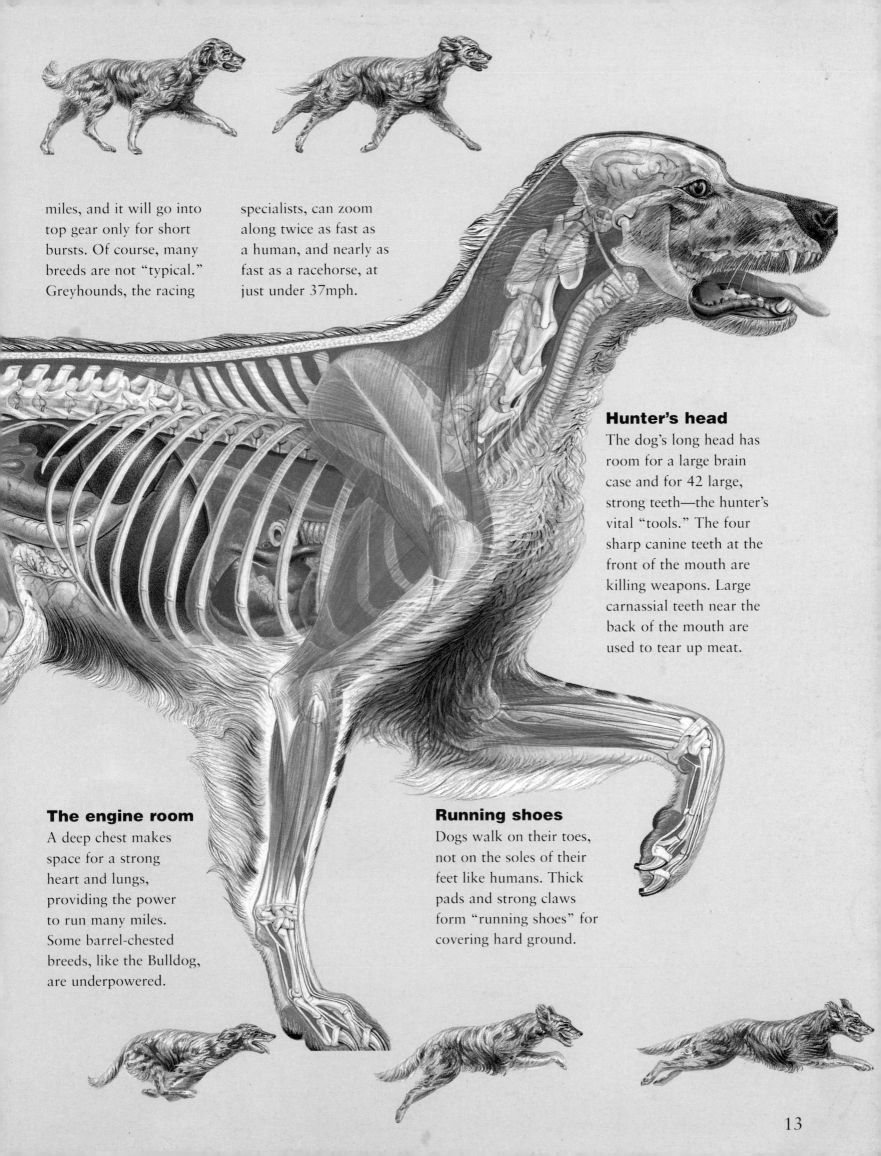

miles, and it will go into top gear only for short bursts. Of course, many breeds are not "typical." Greyhounds, the racing specialists, can zoom along twice as fast as a human, and nearly as fast as a racehorse, at just under 37mph.

Hunter's head

The dog's long head has room for a large brain case and for 42 large, strong teeth—the hunter's vital "tools." The four sharp canine teeth at the front of the mouth are killing weapons. Large carnassial teeth near the back of the mouth are used to tear up meat.

The engine room

A deep chest makes space for a strong heart and lungs, providing the power to run many miles. Some barrel-chested breeds, like the Bulldog, are underpowered.

Running shoes

Dogs walk on their toes, not on the soles of their feet like humans. Thick pads and strong claws form "running shoes" for covering hard ground.

Appearances count

A wild dog's fur is a practical all-weather outfit. It protects the skin and keeps out cold and excess heat. It is really two garments in one: a tough top coat of long, strong guard hairs covering an undercoat of short, softer fur. Some breeds wear the same coat as their wild ancestors. Others have developed more "fashionable" fur—floor-length, crewcut, short, curly, wiry, or even dreadlocked!

Types of coats

The Doberman Pinscher's short, close-lying coat is easy to groom, but others take more work. Rough coats, such as the Border Terrier's, need to be stripped or clipped, while the Afghan's flowing locks and the Puli's cords require constant attention.

Terrier trims
The thick white coat of the West Highland White Terrier, or Westie, needs care. Compare the different styles of the show dog (1) and the clipped pet (2).

1

2

Doberman Pinscher

Afghan Hound

Border Terrier

Puli

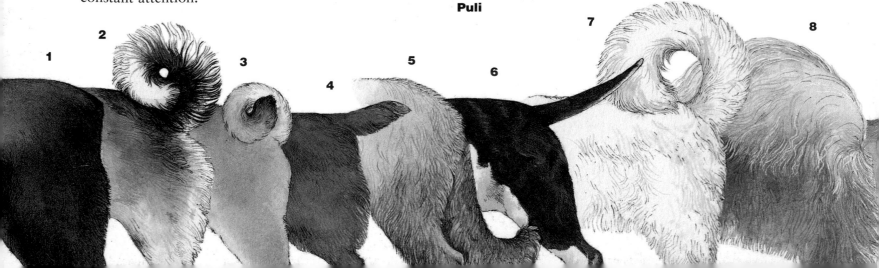

1

2

3

4

5

6

7

8

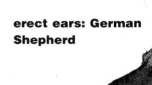

natural ears: wolf

Maxicoat

The Cocker Spaniel has a massive coat, carefully shaped for show dogs (3) and usually clipped for pets (4) for reasons of care and comfort.

Nature designed dogs' ears to stand up in a triangular, funnel shape, which traps and channels sound. But humans have bred dogs with different ear shapes, sizes, and positions. For example, all puppies are born with soft ears, which flop down. By selecting dogs whose ears stay babyish all their lives, we have produced drop-eared domestic breeds such as the Basset Hound.

erect ears: German Shepherd

semi-drop ears: Smooth Collie

rounded bat-ears: Basenji

Curly-coated Retriever

Shar-Pei

The dog's design is adaptable, allowing breeders to develop shapes and styles to suit their fancy. At times they take this too far, breeding coats too heavy for comfort or noses too flat to breathe through. What pleases the human eye may not be good for the dog, so before buying a pup, check to see if the breed has health problems.

drop ears: Basset Hound

pendant ears: Dalmatian

KEY TO TAILS
1 Schipperke (bob tail)
2 Elkhound (single-curled tail)
3 Pug (double-curled tail)
4 Norfolk Terrier (docked tail)
5 Briard (hook tail)
6 Bull Terrier (whip tail)

7 Pyrenean Mountain Dog (plume held high)
8 Pomeranian (plume across back)

9 Pekingese (squirrel tail)
10 Irish Water Spaniel (rat tail)
11 Afghan Hound (ring tail)
12 German Shepherd (saber tail)
13 Chinese Crested (tufted tail)

rose ears: Bulldog

9

10

11

12

13

button ears: Fox Terrier

◄ Hearing varies from breed to breed. Dogs with erect ears can hear better than dogs with floppy ears that cover the ear opening. The least keen hearing belongs to drop-eared breeds, such as Spaniels. But the floppy-eared Afghan Hound—a running hunter—has good hearing because its ears flow back as it runs.

Senses

Dogs see the world differently from humans. Their eyes are not as good at picking out detail, less sensitive to color, but better at spotting movement, and more efficient in dim light. This is because they are hunters' eyes, designed to spot prey—just like dogs' ears, which hear more keenly than ours. Dogs can hear sounds that are inaudible to humans because they are too far away or too high-pitched.

▲ Whiskers above the eyes, on the muzzle, and below the jaws are sensory feelers—less sensitive than a cat's, but still useful as part of a dog's sense of touch.

range of vision for a Pekingese

range of vision for a typical dog

KEY

▤ blind spot
▨ monocular vision (focusing with one eye)
▩ binocular vision (focusing with two eyes)

Dog vision

The range of vision varies from breed to breed, depending on head shape. A typical dog can see through 250°, compared with the 180° of humans and flat-faced dogs like the Pekingese. The area seen by both eyes is in focus. Outside this, one eye picks up movement but not detail.

◄ Termites are the main item on the menu for the Bat-eared Fox. Their huge ears are tuned in to insect footsteps!

A dog uses its keen sense of smell not just for hunting, but for checking its surroundings and communicating with other dogs via scent messages. A dog can read the messages in urine and fecal markers, footprints, and scent particles carried on the air. Although sniffing power varies from breed to breed, the German Shepherd, for example, has 220 million scent cells in its nose—compared to a human's five million.

Smell specialist

Bloodhounds are famed for their keen noses. Like other dogs, they follow both ground scent, made by feet on the ground, and air scent, left hanging in the air after people have gone by. Their sense of smell is so acute, they can follow air scent more than a day after the person has gone. The mystery of mass murderer Jack the Ripper might have been solved if police hadn't abandoned plans to set Bloodhounds on his trail.

Secret senses

Scientists haven't cracked all the secrets of a dog's senses. Somehow Rupert the Border Collie is able to sense when his owner is about to have an epileptic fit and warn her in time to move to safety. She can also rely on him to call an ambulance or bring her the cordless telephone.

newborn puppy

A pile of puppies

Puppies cuddle up close to stay warm. By the time they are about a week old, they are strong enough to crawl around, searching for milk and burrowing into their bedding. Eyes and ears begin to open at about two weeks, but it takes another two or three weeks before they work properly. Sleep and food are the pups' only real concerns at this age.

9–14 days old

Newly born

Newborn puppies are completely dependent on their mothers. Their eyes and ears are sealed shut—they do not need them yet. But their noses work from the start, so they can sniff out their milk supply.

Puppy development

For the first two or three weeks of life, puppies do little but sleep and feed. By about three weeks, most pups have started to take an interest in life and in each other. When they learn to play, at about four weeks, they are starting their schooling—learning how to be dogs. By about 12 weeks, most puppies are able to join in grown-up activities.

The world around

Once eyes, ears, and legs are under control, at about four or five weeks, playtime begins. This is the age when puppies start getting used to the world they will live in as adults. They need to experience normal household noises and activity, and to learn that humans are their friends.

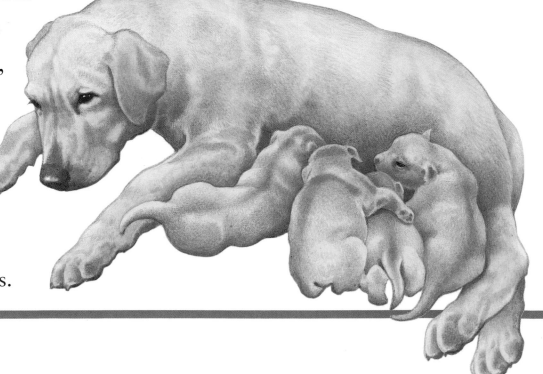

A spotless start

Not all puppies arrive in their adult colors. Yorkshire Terriers are born black, and Dalmatians start out completely spotless! The characteristic spots start to appear when the pups are about two weeks old.

Nursery numbers

The number of puppies born in a litter varies. Small breeds usually have a small litter, perhaps only two or three pups. Large breeds, such as the Great Dane, can produce more than 20 puppies in a litter. Such huge litters are too much for the mother to feed. If all are to live, some pups must be bottle-fed.

A puppy is ready to leave its first home and go to a new owner—somewhere beween six and twelve weeks, depending on the breed. For domestic dogs, it is the key age for a pup to learn about people and attach itself to its new owners.

Mother and pup

The role of the mother is very important in bringing up well-adjusted pups. If she is nervous or snappy, for example, she will pass this on to her offspring.

ALL KINDS OF DOGS

All dogs were mongrels once. Most of the basic types—sheepdogs, hounds, lapdogs, and so on—were established by Roman times. But pedigree breeds as we know them, with every dog of the same breed looking much the same, did not really exist until dog shows began in the 1800s. The demands of the showring soon led to fixed standards of appearance for each breed and then to pedigree breeding as we know it today.

▼ New breeds are still being created. The Eurasier was developed in Germany in the 1950s by crossing the Chow Chow, German Wolfspitz, and Samoyed. An attractive dog, it is not easy to train and is rarely seen outside Germany.

Eurasier

Hunting dogs

Thousands of years ago, humans developed different types of specialist hunting dogs which were faster, stronger, or keener-nosed than the original wolf model. They formed two groups—speed specialists (sight hounds) and nose specialists (scent hounds). Hounds are still important today, often as companions rather than hunters.

▶ In the Middle Ages, hunting with hounds was the sport of kings and noblemen. A royal pack might consist of more than a hundred different kinds of hounds. All were known by name and lovingly tended, and the favorites often slept in the king's bed.

Wire-haired Dachshund

Beagle

Saluki

Hounds at home

Today, many hound breeds are popular pets. The Saluki is favored more as a glamorous companion than as a tough hunter of game, and the Dachshund is so popular as a pet that few realize it began life as a worker, hunting badgers.

▲ Foxhounds were bred for speed and hunting ability. Hunters have always loved the "music" of a pack of hounds baying on the trail and, in the past, even picked hounds for the quality of their voices.

In pre-Roman Britain, small hunting dogs were developed to follow prey underground. Known as terriers (from the Latin word *terra*, meaning "earth"), their small size and cocky temperament make them great companions.

Made in Britain

Most terriers were bred in Britain, as their names imply—Welsh, Irish, Skye. The Cairn is a Scot, named for the rock heaps it hunted through. Other countries now breed their own, such as Germany's Jagdterrier.

Welsh Terrier

Jagdterrier

Cairn Terrier

The nose that knows

The dog's nose has served humans well in hunting and tracking, but has also proven to have more specialist uses. Sporting dogs (originally falconers' dogs) were bred to sniff out game for hunters. Today, working breeds also play a vital role as scent dogs, finding anything from explosives and drugs to lost children and gas leaks.

Rescue dogs

In the 1600s, monks of the St. Bernard's Hospice in the Alps used dogs to find lost travelers. Today, rescue dogs operate around the world. They train with dummies, then real people buried in snow. Modern St. Bernards are too heavy, so German Shepherds and Border Collies now do this work.

Blitz dogs

During World War II, dogs proved better than people at searching bomb sites for the injured and dead. Beauty the Wire Fox Terrier was one canine heroine of the London Blitz. She alone found 63 casualties and was awarded a medal for her war work.

Sporting dogs

The Brittany Spaniel (4) is still a working breed, but the Labrador (2), first bred as a retriever, is now more popular as an assistance dog and pet. The Irish Setter (3) has striking good looks, which have made it a popular pet. It is now rarely seen as a hunting dog. The Bracco Italiano (1), an eager worker, is winning popularity in the showring.

A keen sense of smell, boundless energy, and a kind nature make sporting dogs ideal law enforcement recruits. To them, sniffing out drugs or explosives is a marvelous game—but their skill saves countless lives. One U.S. Customs Service dog, a Golden Retriever, found $60 million worth of smuggled drugs in one year.

On camera

Where humans cannot go, a search dog can—and now it can provide a running report to its handler, thanks to a mini camcorder and microphone mounted on its head. Police and rescue workers use camera-carrying dogs to transmit scenes from earthquakes and terrorist attacks.

To the point

The thrill of the scent locks a Pointer into this rigid position. Even a very young puppy shows this strong drive, pointing at bumblebees in the absence of serious business.

Scent dogs even help in wildlife conservation. Labradors are replacing radio collars for tracking wild animals in the United States. In Britain, Pointers help scientists to find and protect the nests of rare black grouse.

Herding dogs

Looking after livestock may seem like a far cry from hunting them, but it is the wolf's hunting instinct that enables farm dogs to herd sheep and cattle. Owner and dog work together like members of a wolf pack—the dog directs the animals' movements, just as the dog's wild ancestors drove their prey toward their pack mates. Over time, herdsmen bred specialist sheep and cattle dogs which were tough, clever, and had a built-in drive to work. Today, many excel at obedience work. But without plenty of physical and mental exercise, working dogs become bored and destructive.

Hairy hypnotist
The Border Collie is the all-time sheep specialist. Developed to work free-ranging flocks in the wilds of Scotland, Wales, and bordering areas of England, the breed now aids sheep farmers worldwide. Noted for the "strong eye," which it uses to control sheep with an almost hypnotic glare, the Border Collie is highly intelligent and a top obedience breed.

▼ Sheepdogs played a big part in the taming of the Wild West. When the U.S. sheep industry took off in the 1840s (and "range wars" broke out between cattlemen and shepherds competing for good grazing land), Collies were essential for moving flocks several thousand strong. Collies still fulfill this important job all over the world.

▲ Heavy, weatherproof coats are a feature of many European herding breeds, such as this Polish Lowland Sheepdog.

▼ Less well known today than the Collie, the Smooth Collie is an ancient Scottish breed.

▼ Now rarely worked, the Pembroke Welsh Corgi was bred as a cattle dog. Low to the ground, it drove cows by nipping at their heels.

Dog star

Film heroine Lassie is probably the most famous and best-loved dog in the world. She made the Collie a breed everyone knows.

◄ Developed in the 1800s from various Collie types and the native wild dingo, the Australian Cattle Dog is a tough working breed.

Herding dogs were bred in various shapes and sizes to do different jobs. Large, powerful dogs, such as the Maremma, protected flocks from wolves. Small Swedish Valhunds directed stubborn cattle by snapping at their heels, while tough Bearded Collies drove herds hundreds of miles to market. The Shetland Islands, famed for dwarf sheep and ponies, produced a minidog—the Shetland Sheepdog.

Noisy worker

The New Zealand Huntaway is unusual among sheepdogs in that it barks while it works. Driving the sheep from behind, it urges them on vocally.

Beware of the dog

 Just as wolves guard their homes and families, the first dogs turned their keen senses, protective urge, and fighting ability to guarding their human masters—a task performed to this day. At times, they also fought beside their owners in war. By 2000 B.C., the war dogs of Babylon struck fear into opposing armies.

To the rescue

It's not just fierce dogs that protect their owners. Nottie, a gentle Golden Retriever, came to the rescue when his owner was attacked by a herd of cows. By racing for help, he saved his owner's life—and wears his lifesaver's medal with pride.

Dogs in armor

In the Middle Ages, war dogs wore leather and chain-mail armor to attack mounted knights. They were highly effective until the development of gunpowder meant that their armor no longer gave them sufficient protection.

▼ Of these four flock-guarding breeds, only the Bouvier des Flandres and Komondor are likely to be found working in their original role today.

Wherever wolves roamed, or human enemies raided, farmers relied on dogs to protect their flocks and herds. Big, tough, and intelligent, many of these flock-guarding breeds, such as the German Shepherd, are still valued today as protective companions.

Bouvier des Flandres

Rottweiler

German Shepherd

Komondor

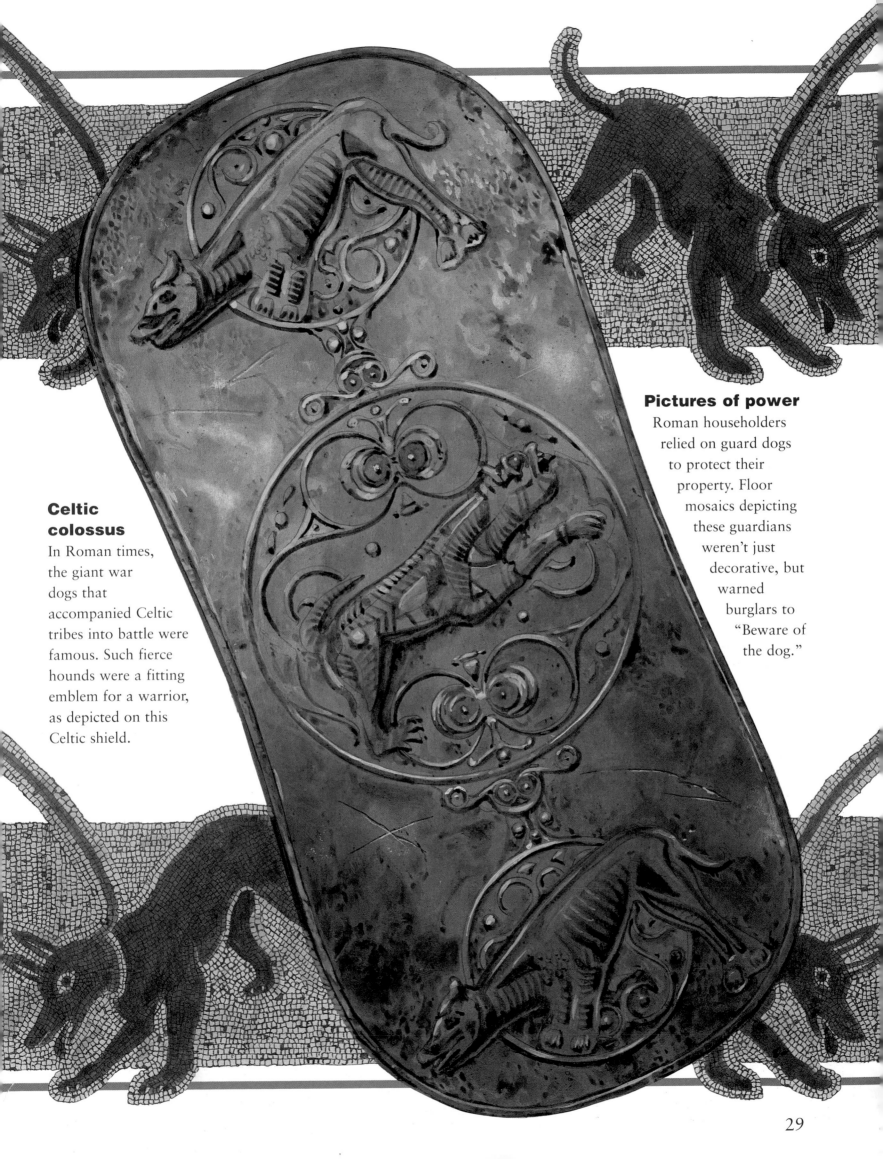

Celtic colossus

In Roman times, the giant war dogs that accompanied Celtic tribes into battle were famous. Such fierce hounds were a fitting emblem for a warrior, as depicted on this Celtic shield.

Pictures of power

Roman householders relied on guard dogs to protect their property. Floor mosaics depicting these guardians weren't just decorative, but warned burglars to "Beware of the dog."

Pulling power

Dogs aren't as strong as horses or oxen, but they are cheaper to keep, so until modern times, dog power was used to pull carts. In the frozen North, sled dogs were invaluable as the only available form of transportation.

Dogged delivery
Dog-powered milk carts were common in 1930s Belgium—cheap and practical transportation for small traders.

▲ In 1911, Roald Amundsen became the first man to reach the South Pole—thanks to the aid of 52 powerful Greenland Huskies. His rival, Captain Scott, lost the race to the Pole largely because he refused to rely on dogs, trusting motorized sleds and ponies instead.

Just for show
Draft dogs were once common in Europe, pulling tradesmen's carts laden with milk, meat, or other goods. Today, Bernese Mountain Dogs pull these beautifully decorated carts for show, no longer laden for work.

Gasoline-powered caterpillar tractors have largely replaced dog power in Arctic regions, and dogsleds are now used only for local transportation—and for the popular sport of sled racing. The most famous race is Alaska's annual 1,200-mile *Iditarod*, but the sport has also spread across Europe. Where snow is scarce. Huskies pull wheeled rigs instead of sleds.

Road dogs

In the 1700s and 1800s, you might have been run over by a speeding dog team. Speed-loving tradesmen, and even disabled beggars who relied on dog power to get around, raced horse-drawn carriages along the road and sometimes won.

Two main groups of dogs are used for transportation: the North's cold-resistant Huskies and western Europe's big, heavy Mastiffs, which usually doubled as guard dogs. Northern sled dogs range from the powerful Alaskan Malamute to the speedy Siberian Husky, as well as the Samoyed, which, in the past, worked as a reindeer herder.

Dragging along

Before horses were introduced by the Spanish, dogs helped the Native Americans to haul their belongings from one camp to another. They were hitched up to *travois* poles—a pair of sticks that trailed behind the dog with the load tied between them.

Hot work

Before modern ovens made life easier, meat roasting over the fire had to be turned to keep it from burning—and dog power provided the easiest method. Small turnspit dogs ran for hours on a treadmill set beside the fire, helping to cook the dinner.

Seeing eyes

Guide dogs give blind people back their independence. The special harness, worn only when the dog is working, lets the owner feel when the dog reaches a step or slope in the path.

Hearing dogs

Hearing dogs for the deaf are trained to alert their owners to all kinds of important sounds, from everyday alarm clocks and doorbells to fire alarms, cooking timers, or crying babies.

Guides and helpers

Dogs have been trained to lead the blind for at least 2,000 years, but we have only recently come to appreciate just how much help a well-trained dog can give its owner. Today, we have not only "seeing eye" dogs for the blind, but "hearing" dogs for the deaf, and even assistance dogs for the disabled.

A helping paw

Assistance dogs help their disabled owners with a wide range of everyday tasks. They carry shopping, fetch objects like cordless telephones, operate buttons for elevators and pedestrian crosswalks, and can even load and unload the washing machine.

Opening doors

People on crutches and in wheelchairs can't open doors very easily, so a canine helper comes in handy. But a support dog also opens the door to an independent life for a disabled owner.

To the rescue

Mountain rescue dogs sniff out lost hikers and avalanche victims, where human searchers are helpless. With its keen sense of smell, and two years' careful training, one dog can do the work of ten men on such missions. Search and rescue dogs have saved many lives, but off-duty they are just normal family pets.

Hospital helpers

Specially trained dogs are welcome visitors in many retirement homes and hospitals. They can sense who needs company or comfort, and sometimes patients who have withdrawn from human contact will respond to a dog's silent sympathy.

Puppy walkers

Puppies bred to be guides and helpers are fostered for their first year by volunteer "puppy walkers" —people who give them basic schooling. This prepares them for specialist training.

Acting as a handicapped person's eyes, ears, or as a helping hand takes a special kind of dog. Golden Retrievers and Labradors are particularly well suited to "the caring professions," but other breeds also serve. Many training organizations breed their own puppies for the job. Others welcome suitable pups donated by breeders or even pick likely-looking recruits from animal rescue shelters. Trainees that don't make the grade as workers are found other homes.

The lap of luxury

Dogs do not have to be workers to be valued. From ancient times, miniature dogs of no practical use were treasured as luxury items by the rich. Their only "work" was to amuse and love their owners. Needing little space and exercise, minidogs are still popular today.

▶ The Papillon (1), Toy Poodle (2), and Cavalier King Charles Spaniel (4) descend from European sporting breeds. The Pug (3) and Shih Tzu (5) are Orientals, and the tiny Chihuahua (6) is a Mexican creation.

Friends at court

Over the ages, lapdogs have been despised as useless by some and adored as comforters by others. The Middle Ages saw small breeds such as the Papillon, Volpino, and King Charles Spaniel established as royal favorites in Europe.

▲ Richard Burton and Elizabeth Taylor are just two of the many film stars who appreciated the fashion for decorative little dogs as pets.

In the East, decorative miniature dogs adorned imperial courts and Buddhist monasteries. China produced short-faced *ha-pa* ("under-the-table") dogs, ancestors of our Pugs, and the "lion dog"—the Pekingese—bred in the image of the Buddhist symbol of the lion.

Man's best friend

Most dogs today don't work for their keep. They are "just pets," although this is not a role to dismiss lightly. Being a companion has always been a major part of the dog's duties. Like his ancestor the wolf, he is a social animal, and his family—canine or human—is important to him. Just as adult wolves will care for cubs that are not their own, many dogs take care of their owners, not only with practical tasks, but also giving comfort and sympathy.

A Welsh hero
Legend says Gelert was babysitting when a wolf attacked. His master came home to see the blood-stained dog by the cradle, misread the signs, and killed his dog. Only then did he discover the baby unharmed beside a dead wolf.

Handle with care
The family dog can be a child's best friend and protector—provided that both child and dog know what they're doing. Many dogs seem to feel a special responsibility for young humans, but true friendship and trust can only grow out of kindness and understanding.

Canine saint

In France, a similar legend was told of the Greyhound Guinefort, who saved his master's child from a great snake. Local people declared the dog a saint—the only dog saint on record. For centuries, his feast day was celebrated on August 22, despite official Church disapproval.

Greyfriars Bobby

In the late 1800s, Bobby the Terrier was a famous Edinburgh character. Now, tourists honor the legend of his faithful watch at his master's grave for 14 years. In real life, he was a pet of the Royal Engineers and haunted restaurants rather than the graveyard.

Countless stories tell just how good a friend the dog has proven to be. One of the earliest appears on a memorial at the Roman city of Pompeii, honoring a dog that saved its child owner's life no less than three times, from water, fire, and robbers. In many lands today, special medals are awarded each year to such canine heroes.

▼ Friendship means doing things together. Mutley, a rescued stray, even joins his owner in scuba diving, wearing his own diving suit. This clever dog also enjoys motorcycle riding, skiing, and tennis.

YOUR DOG

More than any other pet, your dog needs you. Without company and attention, he will be unhappy—and a badly-behaved nuisance. It's up to you to introduce him to your world, and show him how he should behave in it. In fact, the more you help him to enjoy life, the more you will enjoy him!

Language classes

Playing together, these puppies are practicing communication skills— a canine sign language. "Talking" to other pups will help them to understand other dogs when they grow into adults.

Human friends

Meeting strange humans is important, too. Many puppies are shy of strangers, and a puppy class is the ideal place to start making friends.

Gently does it

If your puppy is a little shy, don't try to force him to have fun. Stand back and let him get used to the idea first. Later, he will want to join in.

Pay attention

A good owner never ignores what his puppy is up to. The Spaniel below is picking up bad manners, along with the contents of someone's purse!

Many vets and obedience schools run special sessions for puppies. These "puppy parties" are more play school than training class, and a great way to teach your puppy confidence. If there isn't one in your area, arrange play sessions and short outings for your puppy with friends.

Choosing a dog

Making the choice between male or female, pedigree or mongrel, puppy or adult, is up to you. All can make fine pets. Mongrels are not necessarily healthier, but if you decide on a pedigree, read up on any inherited disorders in the breed, and make sure the breeder has carried out any necessary health tests. Puppies are endearing but hard work; adults may arrive ready-trained, but equally could have some well-established bad habits. Your new friend may be with you for the next ten to twenty years, so choose carefully.

Good home needed

Adopting a dog from a dog pound or shelter can be extremely rewarding. It can also be very hard. Some rescued dogs have had a bad start in life and need experienced new owners to reeducate them. Others have already been loved and trained as delightful companions. Good rescue organizations offer guidance and try to match dogs to suitable owners.

Be careful where you obtain your new friend. Look for a caring breeder or a rescue shelter that works hard at matching dogs to new owners. Expect breeders to interview you thoroughly to make sure you are a suitable owner: it is a bad sign if they don't care where their puppies end up. And don't be afraid to ask questions yourself.

Good homes needed for pups

Golden Retriever puppies, to approved homes only. Raised in home with children. Wormed, registered, and insured. Parents certified in good health by vet. After-sales service.
Tel: 555-9121

DOGS FOR SALE

Yorkie, Poodle, and German Shepherd puppies and adults. Other breeds often available.
Tel: 555-2255

Cute Beagle cross pups, 15 weeks old.
Tel: 555-9071

Choose carefully

Read between the lines in advertisements. "Puppy mills" offer quantity rather than quality. Their puppies are often badly cared for and may never achieve full good health. Nothing can replace the good start supplied by a caring breeder.

Family friends

If you're a first-time dog owner, it's sensible to pick a breed that's easy to live with. Golden Retrievers have a well-earned reputation as reliable family dogs, but do need plenty of exercise and grooming. The Norfolk Terrier is a bundle of fun in smaller form, with typical terrier bounce.

Golden Retriever

Norfolk Terrier

Be sure

Before you buy that appealing pup, make sure you can cope with its adult needs. If you are considering a bouncy Boxer, think about whether you can handle that unruly energy. If you fall for an Old English Sheepdog, will you enjoy all that grooming? The wrong choice may mean misery for both of you.

Old English Sheepdog

Be choosy

Look for a dog that's healthy in mind and body. Some breeds are less outgoing than others, but it's safest to pick a puppy that likes the look of you. Timid or overbold puppies are going to be more challenging, so avoid these two and go for the happy, responsive puppy in the middle.

Boxer

Canine care

 Your dog's practical needs are for food, water, grooming, exercise, and somewhere to sleep. Pet stores stock a bewildering variety of accessories, but you don't need all of them. Either fresh or manufactured food is suitable, but red meat alone does not contain all the vitamins and minerals a dog needs. Fresh water is a must, so keep that water bowl full.

Plain or fancy

Luxury collars, beds, and bowls interest owners more than dogs. A dog will be just as happy with much more basic equipment— as long as the bowl has food in it!

Bedtime

A comfy, draft-proof, and easily-cleaned bed is essential. Avoid beds that can be chewed into sharp edges. A cardboard box may be best for puppies, as it is easily replaced when soiled or chewed. All bedding needs regular flea treatment.

collars and leashes

Taking walks

Your dog needs a collar with address tag and leash. A buckled, leather collar is most comfortable. Choke chains are best avoided: it is all too easy to hurt the dog with these. Dogs that pull may be better with a head collar, which gives you more control. An extending leash can be useful if you can't yet trust your dog off-leash.

Wild dogs care for their own fur, but most pet dogs need help. For short coats, a brisk weekly brushing keeps skin healthy and massages muscles; most long coats need daily care. Heavy-coated dogs, such as the Old English Sheepdog, suffer discomfort after a few days without grooming, and a few months' neglect can mean a trip to the vet. Grooming is a matter of health care, but it is also a way of showing affection and a chance to remind a bossy dog who's in charge.

Brushing

A natural bristle brush suits most types of coats. Work through the whole coat gently, first against the direction of the hair, and then the right way.

Polishing off

For dogs with short to medium coats, finish off by smoothing the fur over with a rubber brush or even a silk cloth to give it a real shine.

Comb with care

Longer hair needs to be combed through to remove tangles, but be careful not to pull the hair. A wide-toothed metal comb is the safest.

Dinnertime

Puppies need several small meals a day; adult dogs need one large meal or two smaller ones, morning and evening. Most dogs will eat more food than is good for them, so keep an eye on your dog's figure.

fresh meat

canned food

biscuits

dried food

mixer biscuits

Playtime

Toys are fun and are also good training aids. But some toys on sale are dangerous. Beware of cheap toys that can be chewed and swallowed, and small balls that can stick in a dog's throat and choke it.

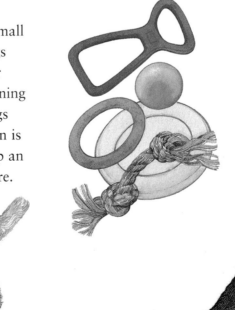

Dog language

Dogs try very hard to understand us, and we can help by trying to understand their sign language of facial expressions, body posture, and voice. A friendly tail wag or a teeth-baring snarl are easily understood, and most owners soon learn to recognize other gestures and expressions. You can tell a lot from a dog's face, and some dogs even learn to copy the human smile, drawing back their lips and showing their teeth just like us.

Who's boss?

Dogs express social status by position: the dominant dog "stands tall," while the submissive underdog grovels. The business of who is top dog and who is underdog is often important in canine relationships. A dog also needs to know in its relationship with its owner whether the dog or the human is "pack leader." Letting the dog be boss doesn't work very well. Knowing that somebody else is in charge makes a dog feel more secure, and therefore easier to train.

Other animals

Dogs don't speak "cat" or any other animal language. When a puppy greets a kitten with a welcoming bounce, the kitten may well think it's being attacked. You will need to introduce your dog to other pets carefully. It takes time and patience to build up friendship between different species.

Let's play

A classic example of the dog's body language, and one of a dog's most charming gestures, is the invitation to play. The dog lowers its front end, while holding its hindquarters and tail high in a posture known as the play bow. The face is relaxed, with an open mouth that looks as if it is laughing. The message is clear: "Come on, let's play!"

Stay away!

Dogs announce their intention to attack with clear signals. The aggressive dog draws itself up to full height, with ears and tail high, bared teeth, and a threatening stare. Even more dangerous is the nervous dog driven to attack by fear: the corners of the mouth are drawn back, the ears flattened, and the tail held low. Always respect a threat display and stay well away.

Saying hello

When you approach a strange dog, the fact that you are taller can look like a threat. Crouch down and offer your hand from a safe distance so the dog can choose to come and investigate. Never approach a dog without asking its owner first!

Messages received by the nose play a large part in communication between dogs. When two dogs meet, they smell each other first, just as we shake hands or say "Hello." Dogs greet us in the same way and learn a lot about us from our scent.

Manners matter

Visitors don't want to be welcomed by a barking dog leaping at the door. Your pet needs to learn to greet people politely—unless they are burglars, of course!

The well-trained dog

Dogs that have been taught how to fit in with our lives are happier and nicer to live with. Most dogs are eager to learn, but sometimes we make it hard for them. Training takes time, patience, and awareness of how dogs see the world. Remember, they don't speak English!

Heel!

Walking a dog that pulls on the leash is no fun for either of you. Puppies learn good manners easily, but you may need help with an older dog that has learned bad habits.

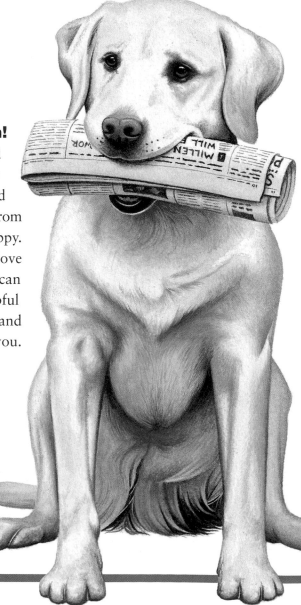

Fetch!

A well-trained dog is a pleasure to live with, and it gets pleasure from making you happy. Hunting dogs love to retrieve, and can be really helpful by fetching and carrying for you.

Digger dogs

Don't leave a new puppy alone in the yard to amuse itself. Stay with it to teach it the rules. Dogs don't know about lawns and roses, but they do know it's fun to dig—unless you teach them otherwise.

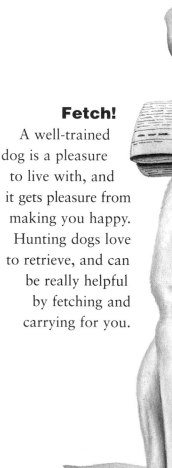

Training classes, where you can learn to train your dog, are offered in most areas. Some teach basic good behavior; others teach competitive obedience, agility, or how to show a dog. A good class is also a social club for your dog, where it can meet friends—and learn not to be distracted by them. It's also a great social club for dog-loving humans!

Ground rules

Military-style obedience isn't necessary in a pet, but reasonable behavior is. Learning to sit, come when called, walk on a slack leash, and stay will ensure your dog doesn't get into trouble.

High jinks

Many dogs enjoy agility training, which involves learning to complete an obstacle course with jumps and tunnels. It's a lot of fun as well as healthy exercise—but not for puppies, who might strain themselves.

Sit!

This is one of the most useful commands. A dog that sits when told is always under control. You can take it anywhere and rely on its behavior being a credit to you.

Best in show

Show dogs have to learn how to behave in the showring—walking nicely, letting the judge examine them, and so on. They also need to learn that showing is fun: a nervous or unhappy dog won't look good enough to impress the judges.

Canine activities

For many people, just having a dog as a companion is enough. But for those who enjoy a challenge, there are plenty of exciting hobbies you can share with your dog. These range from breed shows to obedience training or, for the more energetic, competitive team sports, such as agility and flyball.

Tricks and treats

You may not wish to train your dog to competitive obedience standards, but it can be really fun teaching a dog simple tricks. Most dogs enjoy showing off what they have learned.

Show of skill

Agility competitions are simply obstacle races for dogs. The courses include jumping, climbing, scaling a seesaw, and weaving in and out of a line of poles—all at top speed and with great accuracy. It is great exercise for your dog's body and brain—and yours, too!

Beauty queens—and kings

Breed shows often include special classes for child handlers. It takes careful grooming and hours of training to make the best of your dog.

Flyball

In this popular new team sport, dogs fire tennis balls from a quick-release box, then race to retrieve them—jumping a course of low hurdles on the way.

Terrier racing

Dog racing isn't just for grown-ups with Greyhounds. Other breeds race more informally—and terrier racing can be very informal indeed!

Tunneling away

One of the obstacles on an agility course is the tunnel. An open pipe tunnel like this one is inviting to most dogs. Collapsible cloth tunnels are more challenging. The dog has to find its way, unable to see where it is going.

Whatever your aim, training should be fun for the dog—a hobby it shares with you, rather than a boring lesson. Praise and doggy treats are much more effective than a jerk on the leash and a scolding. Keep lessons short and simple, teach one step properly before going on to the next, and you will find you have an eager pupil.

Seven sleepers

Early Christian legend says seven youths from Ephesus hid from Roman persecution in a mystical 200-year sleep, guarded by their faithful dog Katmir—the only dog admitted to Heaven.

Aztec guide dog

The Aztecs buried a little red or yellow dog with their dead to guide the dead person's soul through the Underworld and over the River of Death.

Three heads

In Roman legend, the world of the dead was guarded by the three-headed watchdog Cerberus. Hercules was the only hero to challenge this guardian successfully.

DOG MYTHOLOGY

The wolf has always lurked on the dark side of mythology, and the legend of the werewolf remains familiar today. The dog's role is less simple. Some ancient religions regarded it as unclean and ungodly, perhaps because of its scavenging habits. But many others honored it as a trusted guardian. From Ancient Egypt, where the jackal-headed god Anubis led the souls of the dead to judgment, to medieval Mexico, where the Chihuahua guided its master's soul across the River of Death, the dog watched over the gateway leading from our world to the next.

▶ Buddhism's lion symbol of a posed a problem to Japanese and Chinese artists unfamiliar with lions. The result was the creation of the Lion Dog, or Fo Dog—part dragon, part Pekingese. Fo Dog statues adorn temples throughout the East. Many wear the tasseled collar and bells traditionally worn by Pekingese at the Chinese royal court.

◄ In Ancient Egypt, Sirius the Dog Star was believed to be the watchdog of the Nile River. The seasonal appearance of Sirius, the brightest star in the sky, announced the coming of the flood season, which gave people time to move to high ground.

Magical dogs

Dogs accompany their masters in legend as in life, playing their role as faithful guardians. Even Noah's ark relied on the dog, which plugged a leak with its nose— and according to legend, this is why dogs have cold, damp noses!

◄ In Egyptian mythology, Sirius the Dog Star is associated with the fertility goddess Isis. The rising of Sirius coincided with the flooding of the Nile. These flood waters brought fertility to the Nile plains and were said to be the tears of Isis weeping for her slain brother Osiris.

Patience rewarded

In Greek legend, the faithful dog Argos waited 20 years for his master Ulysses to return from the Trojan War. When at last the wanderer returned, only Argos recognized him. He licked his master's hand and died content soon after.

Keeping faith

Indian king Yudhishthira refused to enter Heaven without his faithful dog— an "unclean" animal. His loyalty was rewarded, for the dog was actually the god Indra in disguise.

Throughout European mythology, magical packs of hounds stream across the night sky. Sometimes they hunt the Moon, sometimes the souls of men. The leader of the hunt may be a pagan deity, from Greek Artemis to Norse Odin, or a hero, such as King Arthur. In Cornish folklore, he is wicked Squire Dando, who went hunting on the Sabbath and now must hunt forever.

Arthur's hound
Welsh legend says that Britain's legendary King Arthur owned the mighty hound Cabal, who helped him capture the magical boar Twrch Trwyth.

Guardian ghost
At Rose Hill in Maryland, a sinister, blue ghost dog is said to guard the buried gold of his master, who was murdered by thieves in the 1860s.

► When the fairies ride at night, you may hear their red-eared, white hounds baying as they race across the sky— though the less romantic may hear only the hound-like cry of wild geese. The fairy hounds are also the Hounds of Hell, hunting mortal souls.

Canine characters

Dogs play an important role not only in our lives, but also in the world of our imaginations. Since ancient times, writers and artists have created a host of canine images, from the Hound of God to Walt Disney's Pluto. Among them are realistic dogs like those we keep as pets, terrible monsters such as Cerberus, comical dogs like those in James Thurber's cartoons, and dogs used in art as symbols of love and faithfulness—a role they have earned over the centuries.

◀ Medieval dogs loved their comfort just as much as modern dogs! In this Flemish stained glass panel (c. 1450), the luxury of a rich couple's bedroom is underlined by the dog curled in perfect peace at their feet. The dog also serves as a symbol of love between the human couple.

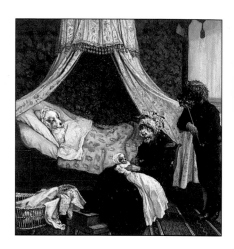

▶ Artists often have fun painting dogs in human clothes and postures. In this painting, *The Newly Born* by J. Stobbaerts (1838-1914), dog family members, with their new puppy, are painted as dog-headed humans—perhaps making the point that family affection is not just a human emotion.

Dogs in art

Paintings and sculptures of dogs through the ages give us some idea of the gradual development of our modern breeds from their wolf-like ancestors. Artists painted real, individual dogs as long ago as the Ancient Egyptian period, but art of all ages also features symbolic dogs and those that are simply decorative. Visit an art museum, and you will be surprised how many human portraits include beautifully painted dogs, often helping to illustrate the character of their owners.

▲ Dogs are a major part of our lives, a fact recognized by many portrait artists who have included the family pets in their compositions. In this portrait of Madame Charpentier and her children by Pierre-Auguste Renoir (1840-1919), the youngsters are surrounded by the protective frame of their mother and the big black-and-white dog.

◀ Painted on limestone, long-legged Egyptian hounds from the New Kingdom period (1555-1080 B.C.) chase off a raiding hyena.

Dogs in literature

The oldest written story about a dog comes from Ancient Greece, and is the tale of faithful Argos in Homer's *Odyssey*. Dogs have featured in our stories, fables, and poems ever since, and many have become well-known and well-loved literary characters in their own right: from Issa, a little lapdog honored by the Roman poet Catullus, to Buck, sled dog hero of Jack London's *Call of the Wild*, or the terrier Boots, in Rudyard Kipling's *Thy Servant A Dog*.

▲ In Geoffrey Chaucer's *Canterbury Tales*, written in the 1300s, the worldly Monk is more fond of hounds and hunting than religious duties. Here, we see him riding with one of his Greyhounds "as swift as a bird in flight."

▲ Sir Arthur Conan Doyle (1859-1930) borrowed from legends of sinister, ghostly hounds in his story of the detective Sherlock Holmes and *The Hound of the Baskervilles*.

▲ In Aesop's fable of "The Dog and the Wolf," the wolf contrasts his own dangerous freedom with the dog's comfortable servitude—and believes he has the better deal.

◄ One of the most popular dogs to have appeared in a comic strip is Snowy, fearless companion of Tintin, both creations of Belgian artist Hergé (1907-83). In 1960, the stories were adapted into an animated TV cartoon.

Dogs in movies and TV

The very first dog star to appear in the movies was Blair, a Collie, hero of the 1905 movie *Rescued by Rover*. He was such a success that a whole series of dogs followed in his footsteps. Early stars included the great German Shepherd Rin Tin Tin; Asta the Fox Terrier in *The Thin Man* series; generations of Collies in "Lassie" movies from the 1940s on; and Scraps the mongrel, Charlie Chaplin's comedy co-star. Today, superbly trained canine actors, such as Benji, earn top dollars.

▲ "Never work with animals or children," says the old show business motto. But Frank Baum's *The Wizard of Oz* wouldn't be the same without Toto the terrier.

◄ Advertisers just love dogs! Many products are closely linked with a particular breed. In Great Britain, the Old English Sheepdog has long been associated with Dulux paint.

Famous dogs

Airedale Jack
World War I messenger dog that saved a British battalion. Cut off under heavy fire, they sent him to HQ with a message asking for reinforcements. Despite horrific wounds, he made the four-mile journey, dying of his injuries as soon as he had achieved his mission.

Antis and his master

Antis
German Shepherd that flew with Czech and British air forces in WWII. He saved lives by detecting the approach of enemy aircraft; rescued people from a bombed house; and saved his master from advancing Communists. Awarded Dickin Medal (British bravery medal for animals).

Balto
Lead dog of the lifesaving marathon relay run in 1925, carrying serum from Anchorage to diphtheria-stricken Nome (Alaska) for 671 miles in freezing 80 mph blizzards.

Barry saves a lost child

Barry
(1800-1812) The most famous of Switzerland's St. Bernard Hospice mountain rescue dogs. He saved over 40 lives.

Becerrillo
War dog that aided the conquistadors of Spain in their conquest of the New World. His name "bull calf" suggests his size.

Black Knight
This famous Pekingese (1945-55) belonged to Lady Munnings and went to every social occasion, including the Coronation of Queen Elizabeth II. He was awarded the Freedom of the City of London and had a book written about him.

Black Knight at table

Bobbie of Oregon
In 1923 Bobbie was separated from his family while on vacation, and they were forced to leave him behind. Bobbie found his way home to Oregon from Indiana. During the 3,000-mile, six-month journey, he crossed three rivers, the Great Plains, and the Rocky Mountains.

Bothie and companions

Bothie
This terrier mascot of the Transglobe Expedition (1979-82) traveled 51,700 miles around the globe. Only dog to visit North and South Poles.

Boy
Prince Rupert of the Rhine's Poodle. He fought beside his master and was said to have supernatural powers. Killed in battle in 1644.

Buddy
"First lady of the Seeing Eye," this German Shepherd was the first U.S. guide dog (1920s). Her success began the guide dogs movement in the U.S.A. and England.

Bullet
Roy Rogers' German Shepherd, and canine TV star of the *Roy Rogers Show* in the 1950s.

Dragon
Dragon's master, Aubry of Montdidier, was murdered in 1371, and the dog's subsequent attack on Richard of Macaire was taken as an accusation. This led to the only case of ordeal by combat between man and dog—Dragon won and Macaire confessed.

Fala
President Franklin D. Roosevelt's Scottish Terrier and constant companion—the first White House pet to be included in a presidential memorial.

Judy on board ship

Igloo
Pet terrier of explorer Admiral Richard E. Byrd and mascot of Anarctica expedition, 1934-35. Flew with Byrd over the North and South Poles.

Judy
The only dog to be officially registered as a Japanese prisoner of war;

British naval mascot from 1936, she spent more than two years in POW camps; awarded Dickin Medal for morale-boosting courage.

Laika in space capsule

Laika

Very first space traveler, launched in Sputnik II (1957). Although she was known as Laika, it is actually the breed name. She was doomed to die in space, as there was no means of bringing her back. In 1998, scientists published a formal apology for sacrificing her life.

Maida

Sir Walter Scott's noble Deerhound-Mastiff, as big as a pony but bullied by Scott's cat; was painted so often that he sighed when he saw an artist coming.

Maida poses for a picture

Nipper

A Fox Terrier painted by Francis Barraud. This portrait became the trademark of RCA, an image which was used for over 50 years after his death in 1875.

Owney

An American traveling dog who rode mail trains around the world on his own, collecting tags from countries he visited.

Patsy Ann

A Bull Terrier whose work in greeting docking ships at Juneau, Alaska, led to her being made Juneau's official greeter in 1934.

Pickles in the limelight

Peritas

Alexander the Great's favorite dog. Traveled with him on great march to India. The dog had a city named in his honor, with a statue in the market square.

Pickles

A mongrel which found the stolen World Cup in 1966 after Britain's top policemen failed.

Pompey, royal savior

Pompey

A Dutch Pug that saved the life of William the Silent in 1572 by alerting him to a nighttime attack. As a result, the breed became associated with the Dutch royal family.

Prince

Irish Terrier-Collie mix, who, during WWII, tracked his master from London across the English Channel to the trenches in France. Thereafter he was adopted by the regiment as their mascot.

Rin Tin Tin

In WWI, U.S. Airmen rescued this German Shepherd puppy from a German dugout in France. Trained to be a police dog in the U.S.A., he was spotted by a movie scout and starred in over 40 silent movies. He received 10,000 letters a week from fans, and died in 1932.

Rob

A World War II para-dog who made over 20 parachute drops into enemy territory and was the most decorated animal in British history.

Roquet

Hound of 1300s that legend says found St. Roche dying of plague in the woods and saved his life by bringing food and licking his sores. The Blessing of the Dogs was held annually on St. Roche's Day, August 16.

Soter

Savior of the city of Corinth in Ancient Greece. The sole survivor after a surprise attack killed 49 of the city's 50 guard dogs, Soter raised the alarm and saved the city.

Trump

The first Jack Russell Terrier, bought by Parson Russell, an avid hunter, in 1819. Trump's successors are now recognized as a popular breed.

Rin Tin Tin

Zeus

This German Shepherd was Korea's first trained rescue dog. His first rescue (saving a lost, car accident victim) hit the headlines early in 1998, was shown on all major TV channels, and appeared in ten major Korean newspapers.

Dog breeds

Domestic dogs evolved from the wolf, but our modern breeds were developed by humans. Dogs with different characteristics were bred together to develop dogs for specific purposes, such as hunting or guarding. Some breeds are now extinct, but new ones are still being developed.

The American Kennel Club recognizes 140 breeds, which are assigned to one of seven groups: sporting dogs, terriers, hounds, toy dogs, nonsporting dogs, working dogs, and herding dogs. Worldwide there are over 400 recognized breeds. Below is a small sampling of dogs from around the world.

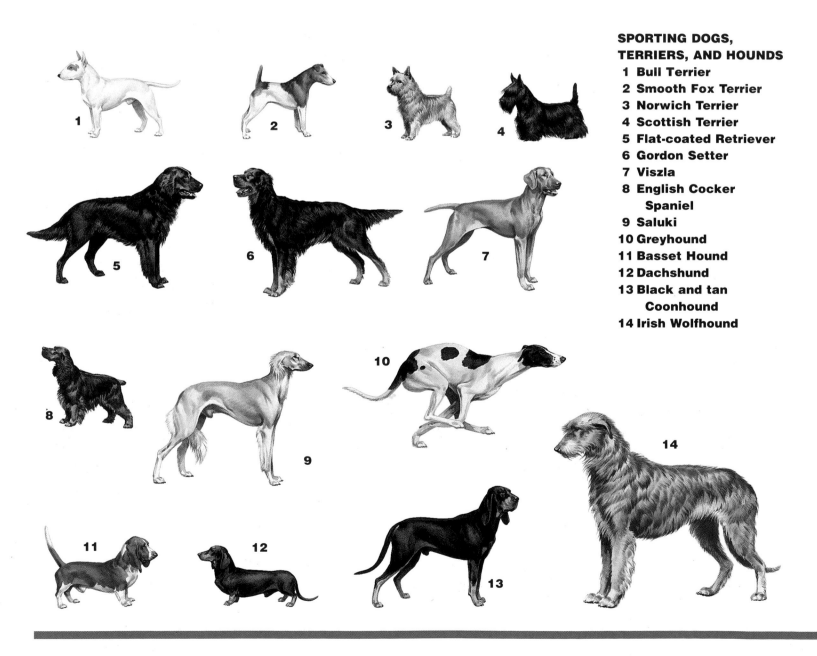

**SPORTING DOGS,
TERRIERS, AND HOUNDS**
1 Bull Terrier
2 Smooth Fox Terrier
3 Norwich Terrier
4 Scottish Terrier
5 Flat-coated Retriever
6 Gordon Setter
7 Viszla
8 English Cocker
   Spaniel
9 Saluki
10 Greyhound
11 Basset Hound
12 Dachshund
13 Black and tan
   Coonhound
14 Irish Wolfhound

**WORKING AND
HERDING DOGS**
15 Neapolitan Mastiff
16 Rottweiler
17 Bullmastiff
18 Great Dane
19 Siberian Husky
20 Samoyed
21 Alaskan Malamute
22 Akita
23 Pembroke Welsh Corgi
24 Shetland Sheepdog
25 Belgian Sheepdog
26 Briard
27 Great Pyrenees
28 Newfoundland

**TOY DOGS AND
NONSPORTING DOGS**
29 Bulldog
30 Dalmatian
31 St. Bernard
32 Elkhound
33 Lhasa Apso
34 Tibetan Spaniel
35 Cavalier King
   Charles Spaniel
36 Bichon Frise
37 Miniature Poodle
38 Löwchen
39 Maltese

Glossary

apple-headed Having a high, domed forehead.

bay Howling call of a hound when hunting.

apple-headed

bench Open-fronted shelf where dogs are secured between classes at some (benched) shows.

bird dog Dog used for hunting birds.

bitch A female dog.

bite How top and bottom teeth fit together when the mouth is shut.

blanket Large patch of color over back and sides.

blaze Broad white stripe running down the face between the eyes.

bloodline A dog's ancestry.

blue Gray coloring ranging from slate gray to pale, bluish gray.

brace Two dogs of the same breed.

breed (1) Class of dogs with similar appearance and related ancestry, e.g., St. Bernard. (2) To mate a male and female dog.

bloodline

breed standards Blueprint by which show dogs are judged.

brindle Color produced by bands of darker hairs on lighter background, giving a striped effect, as on Great Danes.

broken-coated Wire- or rough-haired.

canine (1) Member of the dog family. (2) The long, sharp teeth near the front of the mouth, used for catching and killing prey.

carnassials Ridged, sharp-edged teeth at the back of the mouth, used for gripping and tearing food.

castration Neutering a male by surgical removal of the testes.

cobby Stocky, short-bodied, short-legged, and compact.

condition The state of a dog's health, fitness, and grooming.

conformation Body shape and size, characteristic of a breed.

corded Having a long coat that naturally twines into separate, ribbon-like cords. Seen on Komondors.

corded

coursing Hunting game with sight hounds.

cropping Surgically removing part of the ear to make the remainder stand up. As this is solely for appearance, many vets refuse to do it.

cur A nonpedigree or inferior dog.

dam A mother dog.

dapple Having dark, irregular markings on a lighter background, as on Dachshunds.

dam

dewclaw Claw on inside of the foreleg, somewhat like a thumb.

dewlap Loose skin hanging in folds beneath the throat, as on Bloodhounds.

dock To amputate all or part of the tail. This surgery is performed purely for appearance.

double coat Coat with weatherproof top layer and soft, thick undercoat.

drag An object drawn over the ground to leave a scented trail, to be followed later by hounds.

double coat

dudley nose Pink or light-colored nose.

entire Not neutered.

feathering Fringes of long hair on the belly, ears, backs of legs, and tail.

feral Domestic dog that has turned wild.

flews Long, overhanging upper lips, as on Bloodhounds.

flush To drive game from vegetation.

furnishings Long hair on the head, legs, or tail required by certain breed standards.

gazehound Hound that hunts by sight rather than scent.

grizzled Bluish-gray color of a dog's coat created by a mixture of black and white hairs.

gazehound

guard hairs Long, straight hairs; the top layer of a dog's coat.

hackles Neck hairs that stand up in fear or anger.

hackney action Moving with forelegs raised markedly high.

hard-mouthed Over-rough with retrieved game, marking it with teeth.

harlequin White with black or blue patches, as on Great Danes.

harlequin

haw Membrane at the corner of the eye.

heat Time when a bitch is ready to mate.

hound-marked White with black and tan patches; color pattern typical of hounds.

inbreeding Breeding closely related dogs (such as a brother and sister) together.

incisors Small front teeth, used for nibbling and for grooming.

jowls Hanging fleshy lips and jaws, as seen on Bulldogs.

kennel (1) House for a dog. (2) Boarding house or breeding place.

leather (1) Ear flap. (2) Bare skin of nose around nostrils.

linebreeding Breeding together dogs that are related, but less closely than with inbreeding.

litter Puppies born at the same time to the same mother.

liver Reddish-brown color.

lurcher Hunting dog produced by crossing a gazehound with another working or sporting breed.

mongrel

merle Mottled or marbled color formed by mixture of hair colors.

mixed-breed Dog with parents of different breeds.

molars Large chewing teeth at the back of the mouth next to premolars.

mongrel Nonpedigree dog.

neuter To make an animal incapable of breeding by surgical removal of the reproductive organs.

outcross To breed unrelated dogs together.

overshot Having the upper jaw longer than the lower, so top teeth extend past lower ones.

pack (1) A social unit of wolves or other wild dogs. (2) A number of hounds kept for hunting.

pads Leathery skin on the soles of the paws.

particolor Two or more well-broken colors, one of which must be white.

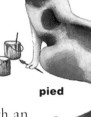

pied Patches of white and another color.

pied

pedigree (1) Purebred dog whose birth has been registered with an official kennel or dog club. (2) Document listing names of the last three to five generations of a dog's ancestors.

point Rigid position in which some dogs freeze when they scent game.

premolars Large chewing teeth between the canines and molars.

puppy Dog under 12 months old.

quick Vein and nerves in a claw.

recognition Official acceptance of a breed for show purposes.

registration Recording a pedigree puppy's birth and parentage.

roan Having colored and white hairs mixed together.

sable Having black-tipped

hairs lying over a lighter background color.

self-colored Having a coat of one color.

sire

show Exhibition of dogs (pedigrees and mongrels). The dogs are judged according to breed standards.

sire A father dog.

soft-mouthed Able to retrieve objects undamaged.

spaying Neutering a female by surgical removal of the ovaries and uterus.

stern Tail of a hound or sporting breed.

stop A marked dent in the bridge of the nose just below the eyes.

studbook A book in which pedigrees are registered.

ticked Speckled with tiny spots of darker color throughout.

tricolor A three-colored dog, usually black, tan, and white.

type Physical appearance of a dog (or breed) in relation to the breed standard.

ticked

undercoat Soft fur under the top hairs.

undershot Having the lower jaw longer than the upper, so bottom teeth extend past the upper ones.

walleye Eye with whitish or bluish iris.

wrinkle Loose folds of skin on the body or head.

wrinkle

Index

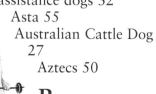

Acknowledgments

The publishers would like to thank the following
illustrators for their contributions to this book:

Mick Brownfield 4-5, **John Butler** 18, **Vanessa Card** 6-7, **Ch'en Ling** 8, **Gino D'Achille**
(Artists' Partners) 8, 24, 30-31, **Peter Dennis** 28, **Sandra Doyle** 12-13, **Ray Grinaway** 46,
47, **Kate Hodges** 60-61, **Sally Holmes** 32-33, **Christian Hook** 26, 29, **Ruth Lindsay** 11,
Angus McBride (Linden Artists) 10, **Malcolm McGregor** 11, 14-15, 20, 22-23, 25, 27,
28, 34, 41, **Danuta Mayer** 22-23, 50-51, 52-53, **Clare Melinsky** 52, 53, **Nicki Palin** 30,
31, 34, 35, 36-37, 51, **Peter Roberts** (Beint and Beint) 36, 38-39, **Mike Rowe** (Wildlife
Art Agency) 19, 44, 45, 48-49, **Claudia Saraceni** 5, 16-17, **Paul Slater** 20-21,
Mark Stewart (Wildlife Art Agency) 40-41, **Helen Ward** (Virgil Pomfret Agency)
9, 14-15, 19, 25, 42, 43, 44.

Appearing throughout the book is Marmaduke the Multifaceted Dog by **Kate Hodges**

The publishers would also like to thank the following for supplying
photographs for this book:

Pages: **9:** NHPA/Stephen Dalton *(br)* **11:** Axel Poignant Archive/Roslyn Poinant *(bc)*
17: Concept @ Charles Barker *(cl)*; Fotomas Index *(br)* **20:** ET Archive *(cl)*
23: Bonhams/The Bridgeman Art Library *(tr)* **24:** Hulton Getty/Fred Morley *(b)*
25: Northamptonshire Police *(cr)* **27:** Ronald Grant Archive *(tr)*; Corbis/Paul A.
Souders *(br)* **28:** Express Newspapers *(tr)* **31:** Mary Evans Picture Library *(br)*
34: Hulton Getty *(cr)* **37:** Frank Spooner/© Gamma *(br)* **38:** Bruce Coleman
Ltd/Jane Burton *(tl)* **40:** RSPCA/Ken McKay *(bl)* **45:** RSPCA/Tim Sambrook *(cr)*
48: Marc Henrie *(cl, bl)*; RSPCA/Ken McKay *(tr)* **49:** Sally Anne Thompson Animal
Photography *(tr, bl)*; Corbis *(cr)* **51:** Private Collection/The Bridgeman Art Library
(br) **54:** ET Archive *(t)*; Berkofine Paintings, Knokker-Zoute, Belgium/The
Bridgeman Art Library *(cr)*; Metropolitan Museum, New York/The Bridgeman Art
Library *(br)*; Louvre, Paris/The Bridgeman Art Library *(bl)* **55:** Frank Spooner/©
Herge/Moulinsart 1998 *(t)*; ET Archive *(tl)*; Mary Evans Picture Library *(bl)*; ET Archive
(bcl); Kobal Collection *(cr)*; Welbeck Golin/Harris Communications Ltd *(b)* **56:** Rex
Features *(cl)*; Popperfoto *(t, c)*; Hulton Getty *(b)*; Corbis *(cr)* **57:** AKG *(tl)*;
Popperfoto *(bl, c)*; Hulton Getty *(tr)*; Kobal Collection *(br)*.

Every effort has been made to trace the copyright holders of the photographs.
The publishers apologize for any unavoidable omissions.

The author would like to thank the following for providing useful information:
Sarah A. Harrison (Song Dog Kennel Europe); Tomlinsons Kennels (Markfield, Leics.) The
publishers would like to thank Tom Frampton of the American Kennel Club for his help.